"Marketing is no longer about the stuff you make but the stories you tell."

— **Seth Godin**

STARTUP HACKS:

70 TIPS TO SLASH MARKETING & DESIGN COSTS WHILE GROWING YOUR BUSINESS

BY HAJRUDIN SPIODIC

For information, contact:
Powered Up Web
contact@poweredupweb.com
www.poweredupweb.com

Cover design by Hajrudin Spiodic
Printed in United States

FOR THE ONES WHO NEVER STOP

To the hard-working mothers and fathers, the entrepreneurs who rise before dawn and stay up late at night, all to feed their kids and put food on the table. This book is for you—the ones who hustle, sacrifice, and pour everything into building a better future. Your perseverance is what drives this book, and your dreams are worth every bit of effort.

And to my incredible clients, who have entrusted PoweredUpWeb with their vision—your trust and belief in what we do have inspired every page of this book. This is for you, as a token of gratitude for your hard work, dedication, and unwavering spirit. May this help you build the future you deserve.

TABLE OF CONTENTS

1. Digital Marketing Hacks ——————————- Page 7

2. Digital Design Hacks ——————————— Page 18

3. Print Marketing Hacks ——————————- Page 29

4. In-Person Advertising Hacks ——————- Page 40

5. Advertising on Apparel Hacks —————— Page 51

6. Vehicle Advertising Hacks ———————— Page 62

7. Business Cards and Postcards Hacks ———- Page 73

8. Final Thoughts - The Road Ahead ———— Page 84

9. Featured Resources ——————————— Page 86

INTRODUCTION

In today's competitive business world, marketing and design are essential for standing out, but they don't have to come with a hefty price tag. Whether you're a small business owner, a freelancer, or a startup, there are countless ways to maximize your impact without draining your budget.

At **PoweredUpWeb**, we've mastered the art of marketing and design, helping clients achieve their business goals through years of experience. We specialize in creating high-quality, cost-effective solutions that make a lasting impact. Beyond delivering exceptional design and marketing strategies, we take pride in advising startups and small businesses on how to cut costs without compromising on quality. With the right approach and the use of modern tools, even the smallest budgets can yield impressive results.

The secret lies in making small tweaks that add up to significant savings. By rethinking your approach and being creative with your resources, you can stretch every dollar and still get the professional results you need. From strategic decisions about how you print your marketing materials to leveraging digital tools, each small step can create a ripple effect of savings and efficiency.

Modern technology, especially AI, has leveled the playing field. With just a few clicks, you can access powerful tools that automate tasks, enhance design, and analyze data—all of which can amplify your marketing efforts without the need for a big budget. This book is packed with actionable tips, hacks, and real-life examples to help you unlock these opportunities and make your marketing work harder for you. Let's dive in and show you how to achieve amazing results—without breaking the bank.

1.
DIGITAL MARKETING HACKS

TIP 1: USE FREE KEYWORD RESEARCH TOOLS TO OPTIMIZE CONTENT

Keyword research is essential for making your content visible online, but it doesn't have to cost you a dime.

Why It Works:

- Free tools like **Google Keyword Planner**, **Ubersuggest**, and **AnswerThePublic** help identify popular search terms.
- Targeting these keywords boosts your website's search engine rankings.

How to Do It:

1. Choose a free tool and search for topics related to your business.
2. Focus on long-tail keywords (phrases with 3+ words) to target specific audiences.
3. Incorporate these keywords naturally into your website, blog posts, and social media.

Real-Life Example:

A bakery in Tampa discovered that "custom birthday cakes near me" was a popular local search term. By using this phrase on their website and social posts, their web traffic increased by 30%. They saved **$1,000** by skipping a paid SEO consultant.

TIP 2: LEVERAGE AI-POWERED PLATFORMS FOR CONTENT CREATION

AI tools like ChatGPT can help you create professional content without hiring a copywriter.

Why It Works:

- AI is fast, efficient, and affordable.
- Tools like ChatGPT, Jasper, and Writesonic can draft:
  - Social media captions
  - Blog posts
  - Email newsletters

How to Do It:

1. Sign up for a free or low-cost AI tool.
2. Input prompts like "Write a friendly Instagram caption for a summer sale."
3. Edit the output for a personal touch.

Real-Life Example:

A boutique clothing store used ChatGPT to draft product descriptions and Instagram captions. Over a year, they saved **$3,000** in copywriting fees while maintaining a professional image.

TIP 3: SCHEDULE POSTS IN BULK WITH AFFORDABLE TOOLS

Consistency on social media is key, but managing daily posts can be a hassle.

Why It Works:

- Tools like **Buffer**, **Hootsuite**, and **Later** allow you to pre-schedule posts.
- Saves time and ensures consistent posting.

How to Do It:

1. Spend an hour each week scheduling posts.
2. Use built-in analytics to identify the best posting times.
3. Use templates for quick and easy post creation.

Real-Life Example:

A fitness coach scheduled a month's worth of Instagram posts using Buffer for $15/month. The result? A **50% increase in engagement** and **$2,500 saved** by not hiring a social media manager.

TIP 4: CREATE FREE LANDING PAGES WITH CARRD OR MAILCHIMP

Landing pages are vital for promoting products or capturing leads, but custom-built pages can be pricey.

Why It Works:

- Platforms like **Carrd** and **Mailchimp** let you build professional landing pages for free.
- Great for promoting events, freebies, or specific products.

How to Do It:

1. Choose a template that matches your goal.
2. Add your content and a strong call to action (CTA).
3. Publish your page and share it on your channels.

Real-Life Example:

A freelance designer used Carrd to create a simple portfolio page. The cost? $0. The result? Five new clients in three months, saving **$1,500** on web development fees.

TIP 5: USE USER-GENERATED CONTENT (UGC)

Why pay for influencers when your customers can become your marketers?

Why It Works:

- UGC is authentic and relatable.
- People trust content from fellow consumers more than ads.

How to Do It:

1. Create a branded hashtag (e.g., #MyCoffeeMoment).
2. Encourage customers to share photos or reviews featuring your product.
3. Repost their content on your social channels.

Real-Life Example:

A coffee shop ran a campaign asking customers to share their latte art using a branded hashtag. The campaign generated **200 new followers** and saved **$800** on influencer marketing.

TIP 6: RUN A/B TESTING ON ADS

Stop guessing which ads will perform best—test them instead!

Why It Works:

* A/B testing compares two versions of an ad to see which gets better results.
* Helps you optimize ad spend for maximum ROI.

How to Do It:

1. Create two variations of the same ad.
2. Test different elements (e.g., headline, image, or CTA).
3. Analyze results and scale the better-performing ad.

Real-Life Example:

An online boutique ran A/B tests on Facebook Ads, finding that text-focused ads converted better than image-heavy ones. They saved **$1,200** by avoiding underperforming ads.

TIP 7: LEARN BASIC SEO TECHNIQUES

SEO might seem complex, but free resources make it accessible.

Why It Works:

- Basic SEO can dramatically increase website traffic.
- Small changes, like optimizing images or meta descriptions, go a long way.

How to Do It:

1. Watch free tutorials on YouTube or platforms like Coursera.
2. Apply what you learn to your website step by step.
3. Use free tools like Yoast SEO for WordPress sites.

Real-Life Example:

A photographer optimized their website's images and alt text after watching SEO tutorials. Traffic increased by **40%**, and they saved **$2,000** on hiring a consultant.

TIP 8: COLLABORATE WITH OTHER BUSINESSES FOR CO-PROMOTIONS

Teamwork can save you money and multiply your reach.

Why It Works:

- Shared promotions reduce individual costs.
- Partners can help you reach new audiences.

How to Do It:

1. Identify businesses with similar audiences but no direct competition.
2. Plan a joint giveaway, event, or promotion.
3. Share marketing duties and expenses.

Real-Life Example:

A pet groomer partnered with a pet store for a social media giveaway. Each business contributed $50 in prizes, gaining **500+ followers each** and saving **$1,000** on ad spend.

TIP 9: AUTOMATE LEAD GENERATION WITH TOOLS LIKE ZAPIER

Let automation handle the boring stuff.

Why It Works:

- Saves time by syncing apps like Facebook Lead Ads and Google Sheets.
- Reduces the need for manual data entry.

How to Do It:

1. Set up a Zapier account.
2. Connect lead capture tools to your CRM or spreadsheet.
3. Watch as leads flow in automatically!

Real-Life Example:

A real estate agent automated lead collection, saving 10 hours weekly and **$8,000 annually** on assistant wages.

TIP 10: RUN COST-EFFECTIVE RETARGETING CAMPAIGNS

Get more conversions by targeting warm leads.

Why It Works:

- Retargeting focuses on people who've already interacted with your brand.
- These audiences are more likely to convert.

How to Do It:

1. Set up a retargeting campaign on Facebook Ads Manager.
2. Use custom audiences based on website visitors or social media interactions.
3. Test small budgets first ($5-$10/day).

Real-Life Example:

A skincare brand spent $100 on retargeting ads, generating **$1,200 in sales** while avoiding wasted spending on cold leads.

2.
DIGITAL DESIGN HACKS

TIP 1: USE FREE OR LOW-COST DESIGN TOOLS LIKE CANVA FOR PROFESSIONAL GRAPHICS

Creating professional designs doesn't require hiring a graphic designer or purchasing expensive software.

Why It Works:

- **Canva** offers an easy-to-use platform with tons of templates for everything from social media posts to brochures.
- With free and affordable premium options, Canva is perfect for startups on a budget.

How to Do It:

1. Sign up for a free account on Canva.
2. Browse templates and select the one that suits your needs.
3. Customize the design with your brand colors, logo, and text.

Real-Life Example:

A small café owner used Canva to design eye-catching social media posts, menu boards, and flyers. They saved **$2,000** by not hiring a designer, and the high-quality designs boosted their social media following by **25%**.

TIP 2: EXPERIMENT WITH AI DESIGN TOOLS LIKE LOOKA OR DESIGNIFY FOR LOGOS AND BRANDING

AI design tools make logo and branding creation simple and affordable for anyone.

Why It Works:

- **Looka** and **Designify** use AI to generate logos and branding elements quickly based on your preferences.
- These tools can help you get started without the high cost of custom design services.

How to Do It:

1. Visit **Looka** or **Designify** and input your business name and industry.
2. Select a few design preferences (e.g., colors, styles).
3. Download the logo files and tweak them as needed.

Real-Life Example:

A startup tech company used **Looka** to create a professional logo in 30 minutes for just **$50**. The process would have otherwise cost them **$1,000** if they had hired a designer.

TIP 3: UTILIZE FREE STOCK PHOTO WEBSITES LIKE UNSPLASH OR PEXELS

Hiring photographers or purchasing stock photos can be expensive, but free stock photo websites provide a wealth of high-quality images.

Why It Works:

- **Unsplash** and **Pexels** offer thousands of free, high-resolution images that can be used commercially.
- Save money while still getting professional-quality visuals.

How to Do It:

1. Search for relevant images on **Unsplash** or **Pexels**.
2. Download images and use them in your marketing materials.
3. Always check licensing terms to ensure proper usage.

Real-Life Example:

A local fashion brand used free images from **Pexels** in their online store and marketing emails. This saved them **$500** in photography fees while still presenting a polished, professional look.

TIP 4: REUSE AND REPURPOSE YOUR DESIGNS FOR DIFFERENT PLATFORMS

Repurposing designs across multiple platforms helps you get more value from your creative work.

Why It Works:

- A single design can be adapted for different formats like Instagram posts, Facebook banners, and email headers.
- Reduces the need for creating entirely new designs from scratch.

How to Do It:

1. Create a core design (e.g., a poster or social media graphic).
2. Resize and adjust it for other platforms using tools like Canva's built-in resizing feature.
3. Ensure the design still works for the new format and audience.

Real-Life Example:

An online fitness coach created a workout challenge graphic and repurposed it across Instagram, Facebook, and their email newsletter. This saved them **$1,500** on additional design work.

TIP 5: CREATE CUSTOMIZABLE TEMPLATES FOR RECURRING DESIGNS

Streamlining your design process with reusable templates can save you tons of time and money.

Why It Works:

- By creating templates for recurring design needs (like social media posts or newsletters), you can keep your branding consistent without starting from scratch every time.
- Templates are quick to edit and customize, reducing the need for frequent design work.

How to Do It:

1. Create a template for your most common design tasks (e.g., Instagram posts, email headers).
2. Save the template in a design tool like Canva or Adobe Spark.
3. Use it regularly, making minor adjustments to fit the new content.

Real-Life Example:

A startup fashion brand created a template for Instagram stories promoting sales. By reusing the template weekly, they saved **$2,000** in designer fees and kept their content looking cohesive.

TIP 6: LEARN BASIC GRAPHIC DESIGN SKILLS THROUGH FREE PLATFORMS LIKE CANVA DESIGN SCHOOL

Learning some basic design skills can make a world of difference in creating your own high-quality visuals.

Why It Works:

- **Canva Design School** offers free courses on design basics like color theory, typography, and layout.
- Understanding design principles helps you create better content that aligns with your brand.

How to Do It:

1. Sign up for free courses on **Canva Design School**.
2. Focus on key areas like color schemes, alignment, and font pairings.
3. Apply your newfound knowledge to your designs.

Real-Life Example:

A small e-commerce business owner took a few basic design courses on Canva Design School. Afterward, they improved the look of their product images and website design, increasing sales by **20%**. They saved **$1,500** by not outsourcing the design work.

TIP 7: OUTSOURCE ONE-TIME DESIGN NEEDS TO AFFORDABLE FREELANCERS ON FIVERR OR UPWORK

If you need something beyond your skills but don't want to break the bank, freelancers can be a great solution.

Why It Works:

- Platforms like **Fiverr** and **Upwork** offer affordable freelancers who can tackle one-time design projects, like logo creation or website graphics.
- You can find designers with different levels of experience and price points.

How to Do It:

1. Browse **Fiverr** or **Upwork** to find designers who fit your needs.
2. Look at their portfolios and read reviews before hiring.
3. Set clear expectations for what you need, including file formats and deadlines.

Real-Life Example:

A small startup hired a freelance logo designer on **Fiverr** for $100 instead of paying a $1,500 fee to an agency. The freelancer delivered a high-quality logo that helped the brand attract more attention.

TIP 8: USE AI-BASED PHOTO ENHANCERS FOR BETTER IMAGE QUALITY

If your images look dull or blurry, AI-based photo enhancers can help bring them to life.

Why It Works:

- **Adobe Express** and similar tools use AI to enhance image quality, improve resolution, and remove imperfections.
- These tools are affordable and often provide free versions.

How to Do It:

1. Upload your images to **Adobe Express** or a similar platform.
2. Let the AI adjust the image quality automatically.
3. Download the enhanced image for use in your marketing materials.

Real-Life Example:

A fashion retailer used **Adobe Express** to enhance their product photos for online listings. This saved **$500** that would have been spent on professional photo retouching.

TIP 9: KEEP BRANDING CONSISTENT TO MINIMIZE DESIGN REVISIONS

Consistency is key when it comes to building a strong brand identity.

Why It Works:

- Maintaining consistent branding across all your materials (logos, colors, fonts) minimizes confusion and creates a cohesive experience for your customers.
- Reduces the number of revisions needed, saving both time and money.

How to Do It:

1. Create a branding guide that includes your logo, color palette, typography, and imagery style.
2. Stick to this guide for all your design projects.
3. Regularly review your brand materials to ensure consistency.

Real-Life Example:

A local restaurant implemented a branding guide for their menu, website, and social media. This saved them **$1,000** by minimizing design revisions, as everything adhered to the established style.

TIP 10: BATCH DESIGN PROJECTS TO SAVE TIME AND MONEY

Rather than designing one piece at a time, batching your design tasks helps you stay organized and efficient.

Why It Works:

- Working on multiple designs at once eliminates the time spent on switching between tasks.
- It also allows for greater creative consistency across projects.

How to Do It:

1. Set aside specific times to design in bulk (e.g., create all your social media posts for the week).
2. Group similar tasks together, like editing photos or updating your website.
3. Use design templates to speed up the process.

Real-Life Example:

A content creator set aside one afternoon per week to batch design YouTube thumbnails, blog graphics, and social media posts. This saved them **$1,500** by eliminating the need for a full-time designer.

3.
PRINT MARKETING HACKS

TIP 1: PRINT IN BULK TO SAVE ON PER-UNIT COSTS

Printing in bulk is one of the most effective ways to reduce the cost per unit and maximize your marketing budget.

Why It Works:

- The more units you print, the lower the cost per piece, making it a great strategy for high-volume marketing materials.
- This approach is ideal for materials like flyers, brochures, and postcards that you plan to distribute over time.

How to Do It:

1. Determine how many units of each print piece you'll need for the next few months.
2. Get quotes from local and online printers to compare bulk pricing.
3. Opt for larger print runs to reduce the overall cost.

Real-Life Example:

A local coffee shop printed 5,000 flyers in bulk instead of 500, which lowered their per-unit price from **$0.50** to **$0.25**. The shop saved **$1,250**, allowing them to distribute flyers more widely.

TIP 2: USE LOCAL PRINTERS TO AVOID HIGH SHIPPING FEES

Shipping fees can add up quickly, especially when you need large print runs.

Why It Works:

- Local printers save you shipping costs, and you can often pick up the print materials directly, saving both money and time.
- You can also support local businesses and potentially negotiate discounts or faster turnaround times.

How to Do It:

1. Research local printers in your area and request quotes for your print projects.
2. Compare pricing with online printers, but factor in shipping fees to see the full cost.
3. Arrange pickup if it's more cost-effective than having items shipped.

Real-Life Example:

A small business selling handmade jewelry used a local printer for their business cards and brochures. They saved **$200** in shipping fees compared to using an online service, and the faster turnaround time allowed them to get their materials in-hand within 2 days.

TIP 3: TAKE ADVANTAGE OF DISCOUNTS AND PROMOS FROM ONLINE PRINTERS LIKE VISTAPRINT

Online printers frequently run sales or promotions that can significantly reduce the cost of print marketing materials.

Why It Works:

- **Vistaprint**, **Moo**, and other online printers offer regular discounts, promo codes, and bulk deals, making it easy to get quality prints at a fraction of the price.
- Signing up for newsletters or checking social media accounts for special offers can also help you stay ahead of seasonal sales.

How to Do It:

1. Sign up for email alerts or follow online printers on social media.
2. Plan your print needs around the sale cycles.
3. Use promo codes at checkout for extra savings.

Real-Life Example:

A small online clothing store signed up for Vistaprint's newsletter and took advantage of a 40% off coupon for their business card order. They saved **$300** on 5,000 cards, which helped stretch their marketing budget further.

TIP 4: CHOOSE SIMPLE, ELEGANT DESIGNS TO MINIMIZE PRINTING COMPLEXITY AND COSTS

The more complex the design, the higher the printing cost due to the need for special colors, cuts, or finishes.

Why It Works:

- Simple designs are cheaper to produce because they require less ink, fewer colors, and often less intricate printing techniques.
- An elegant, minimalist design can be just as effective as a complicated one.

How to Do It:

1. Opt for fewer colors or basic designs that still align with your brand.
2. Focus on clean lines and easy-to-read typography.
3. Consider using flat colors instead of gradients or special effects.

Real-Life Example:

A new restaurant created simple, elegant flyers featuring just their logo, contact info, and an appetizing image. The minimal design cut printing costs by **30%**, saving **$400** on their initial flyer run.

TIP 5: USE QR CODES TO REDUCE THE NEED FOR LENGTHY BROCHURES

QR codes are a low-cost way to provide additional content without the need for large, expensive print materials.

Why It Works:

- Instead of printing a lengthy brochure, you can use a QR code to link directly to your website, product pages, or a video that provides more information.
- QR codes are simple to create, often free, and can be scanned from mobile devices.

How to Do It:

1. Use a free tool like **QR Code Generator** to create your QR code.
2. Place the code on your marketing materials (e.g., business cards, posters, flyers).
3. Ensure the linked content is mobile-friendly and easy to access.

Real-Life Example:

A travel agency included a QR code on their flyer, which linked to a video showcasing popular vacation packages. This saved them **$500** in printing costs by eliminating the need for a 10-page brochure, while the QR code helped increase customer engagement by **40%**.

TIP 6: PARTNER WITH NON-COMPETING BUSINESSES TO SHARE FLYER OR POSTER SPACE

Collaborating with other businesses in your area can help you share marketing costs.

Why It Works:

- By partnering with complementary businesses (like a gym and a health food store), you can split the cost of printing flyers or posters and reach a wider audience.
- Shared flyers or posters allow you to target multiple customer bases without increasing your marketing budget.

How to Do It:

1. Identify local businesses that cater to a similar target audience but aren't direct competitors.
2. Agree to split the cost of printing flyers, posters, or handouts.
3. Distribute materials in both businesses' locations.

Real-Life Example:

A yoga studio partnered with a nearby health food store to share the cost of printing 1,000 flyers. Each business added its information, which helped them double their exposure and save **$250** on printing.

TIP 7: USE AI TO CREATE STRIKING TYPOGRAPHY DESIGNS FOR PRINT

AI tools can help you create bold, eye-catching typography that makes your print materials stand out.

Why It Works:

- AI design platforms like **Looka** or **Canva** can automatically generate attractive typography based on your brand style, reducing the time and effort spent on design.
- These tools also allow for easy experimentation with different fonts and layouts to find the most effective design.

How to Do It:

1. Use an AI-based design tool like **Looka** to generate typography for your print materials.
2. Customize the design by adjusting font sizes, spacing, and colors.
3. Use this typography on flyers, posters, and business cards.

Real-Life Example:

A startup used **Looka** to generate a custom typography design for their flyer. The AI-generated design stood out in a competitive market, leading to a **15%** increase in event signups and saving **$300** on a professional designer.

TIP 8: FOCUS ON EVERGREEN CONTENT THAT DOESN'T REQUIRE FREQUENT UPDATES

Instead of printing time-sensitive materials, focus on content that remains relevant for longer periods.

Why It Works:

- **Evergreen content**—such as general business information, special offers, or services—doesn't require constant revisions, saving you the cost of reprinting.
- Materials like business cards, brochures, and posters can be reused for a longer time.

How to Do It:

1. Identify content that is timeless, such as your company's mission, core services, or brand story.
2. Avoid promoting specific events or sales unless they're long-term.
3. Print materials with a focus on evergreen messaging.

Real-Life Example:

A local law firm printed brochures with information on their services and expertise. The brochure was used for over a year without needing updates, saving them **$1,000** in reprinting costs.

TIP 9: PROOF EVERYTHING TWICE TO AVOID COSTLY REPRINTS

Mistakes in your print materials can be expensive to correct, so it's crucial to double-check everything before sending it to print.

Why It Works:

- Small errors like typos, incorrect phone numbers, or misspelled brand names can lead to the need for costly reprints.
- Proofreading multiple times ensures that your materials are flawless before production begins.

How to Do It:

1. Proofread your designs for accuracy, spelling, and grammar.
2. Have someone else review the materials for a fresh perspective.
3. Double-check important details like URLs, phone numbers, and addresses.

Real-Life Example:

A company printed 5,000 brochures without properly proofreading, leading to a minor typo in the contact information. The reprints cost them **$600**, which could have been avoided with better attention to detail.

TIP 10: USE RECYCLED MATERIALS TO SAVE MONEY AND PROMOTE SUSTAINABILITY

Using recycled materials for your print marketing helps cut costs and promotes an eco-friendly image.

Why It Works:

- **Recycled paper** and **eco-friendly materials** are often less expensive than their non-recycled counterparts.
- By using sustainable materials, you can also attract environmentally conscious customers.

How to Do It:

1. Ask your printer if they offer recycled or eco-friendly paper options.
2. Choose recycled materials for business cards, brochures, or other print materials.
3. Highlight the sustainability aspect in your messaging.

Real-Life Example:

A retail store switched to recycled paper for their flyers and business cards, saving **15%** on printing costs.

4.
IN-PERSON ADVERTISING HACKS

TIP 1: OFFER REFERRAL DISCOUNTS INSTEAD OF PRICEY BILLBOARD ADS

Billboard advertising can be expensive and offers no direct way to track customer engagement. Instead, use a referral discount program to incentivize your existing customers to spread the word.

Why It Works:

- **Referral programs** can be highly effective, with customers acting as your ambassadors and bringing in new business.
- Unlike billboard ads, you can track referrals and reward customers for bringing in new clients, ensuring that your advertising dollars are spent efficiently.

How to Do It:

1. Offer a **discount or bonus** for customers who refer new clients to your business.
2. Set clear terms for the referral program (e.g., give a 10% discount for each referral).
3. Track referrals using software like **ReferralCandy** or manually through an online form.

Real-Life Example:

A local salon replaced their billboard ads with a referral program, offering a 15% discount for every new customer referred. This strategy brought in 30 new clients in the first month, saving them **$1,200** compared to the cost of billboard ads, which would have been a one-time exposure.

TIP 2: USE CREATIVE, LOW-COST PROPS LIKE CHALKBOARDS OR BANNERS AT EVENTS

Instead of spending a lot of money on high-end displays, consider using simple props like chalkboards, banners, or signs to catch people's attention.

Why It Works:

- Chalkboards or banners are budget-friendly and easy to customize.
- They can also create a more personal and inviting atmosphere at events, helping to engage potential customers.

How to Do It:

1. Buy a few **chalkboards** or **banner stands** from a local store or online.
2. Use them to display key information, promotions, or fun messages to passersby.
3. Be sure to keep the design clean, simple, and on-brand.

Real-Life Example:

A food truck at a local festival used a chalkboard to advertise daily specials, which drew in more foot traffic. They spent **$40** on the board, but it helped boost sales by **15%**, an estimated extra **$500** during the event.

TIP 3: NEGOTIATE SPONSORSHIPS FOR LOCAL EVENTS TO GET YOUR LOGO FEATURED

Sponsorships can often be more affordable than traditional ads, and they offer the added benefit of exposure at community events.

Why It Works:

- Local event sponsorships often come with perks like having your logo featured on signage, promotional materials, and even event t-shirts.
- Sponsoring an event helps build goodwill in the community and positions your business as a local supporter.

How to Do It:

1. Research local events in your area (like fairs, festivals, or charity runs) that align with your target audience.
2. Reach out to event organizers to negotiate a sponsorship package that fits your budget.
3. Ask for visibility on printed materials, event signage, and social media.

Real-Life Example:

A local gym sponsored a charity 5k run for **$300**, and in return, their logo was featured on race t-shirts, banners, and in the event's social media posts. The exposure led to a **20%** increase in memberships, which helped recover the cost and then some.

TIP 4: USE PORTABLE BANNERS AND DISPLAYS YOU CAN REUSE

Portable banners are a cost-effective way to create professional displays that you can use at various events.

Why It Works:

- **Retractable banners** and **pop-up displays** are lightweight, easy to transport, and can be used repeatedly at different events.
- They save you money on new display materials each time you attend an event.

How to Do It:

1. Purchase a **retractable banner** or **pop-up display** from a trusted supplier like **Vistaprint** or **BannerBuzz**.
2. Customize the banner with your brand's logo, message, and call to action.
3. Reuse the banner at every event you attend.

Real-Life Example:

A home improvement business bought a retractable banner for **$150** and used it at **5 events**. They were able to advertise consistently without additional display costs, helping them save **$500** compared to printing new signs for each event.

TIP 5: DIY EVENT BOOTHS WITH BUDGET-FRIENDLY MATERIALS

Setting up a booth at local events can be expensive, but with a little creativity, you can build an attractive booth without breaking the bank.

Why It Works:

- Building your booth from scratch gives you complete control over design and cost.
- You can use budget-friendly materials like PVC pipe, foam board, or fabric to create a professional-looking display.

How to Do It:

1. Look for inexpensive building materials such as **PVC pipes**, **foam boards**, and **fabric** for table covers or banners.
2. Consider **DIY tutorials** online for creating simple, yet effective booth structures.
3. Personalize the booth with **branded materials**, such as your logo, flyers, and giveaways.

Real-Life Example:

A small business spent **$100** to build a simple booth using PVC pipes and fabric. They participated in **4 local events** and reached over **500 potential customers**, saving them approximately **$1,000** compared to renting a booth space or paying for a professional setup.

TIP 6: GIVE OUT BRANDED STICKERS OR INEXPENSIVE SWAG INSTEAD OF PRICIER ITEMS

Instead of spending a fortune on high-end promotional items, opt for **branded stickers**, pens, or other low-cost giveaways.

Why It Works:

- Inexpensive items like stickers or pens are still useful and can serve as a constant reminder of your business.
- They're lightweight and easy to distribute at events, which can lead to better ROI.

How to Do It:

1. Choose a promotional item that is both **affordable** and **useful**.
2. Customize the item with your **logo** and a **call to action**.
3. Give them away at events, trade shows, or in-store promotions.

Real-Life Example:

A clothing boutique handed out branded stickers at a local market. They spent **$50** on 500 stickers, which led to increased traffic to their store and a **10%** sales boost.

TIP 7: USE AI TO ANALYZE FOOT TRAFFIC DATA AND IDENTIFY THE BEST EVENT LOCATIONS

Foot traffic data can help you identify high-traffic locations for your in-person events, ensuring you maximize your exposure.

Why It Works:

- By using **AI-powered tools** to analyze foot traffic patterns, you can choose event locations with the highest potential customer engagement.
- This helps you avoid low-traffic areas and save on booth space or event fees.

How to Do It:

1. Use AI platforms like **Geospatial Intelligence** or **Placer.ai** to get foot traffic data.
2. Identify areas with high foot traffic that match your target demographic.
3. Choose events or locations accordingly for the best ROI.

Real-Life Example:

A tech startup used foot traffic data from **Placer.ai** to select events with the highest foot traffic. This strategy helped them increase lead generation by **25%** without spending extra money on low-traffic events.

TIP 8: ENGAGE WITH YOUR AUDIENCE DIRECTLY FOR BETTER ROI ON YOUR ADVERTISING SPEND

Engaging directly with your audience at events ensures you make a lasting impression.

Why It Works:

- In-person interactions allow you to create a **personal connection**, which leads to higher engagement and conversion rates.
- Direct engagement can result in stronger leads and better word-of-mouth referrals.

How to Do It:

1. **Smile**, make eye contact, and ask questions to engage with people at events.
2. **Explain** your products or services clearly, and answer questions in a friendly and approachable way.
3. **Follow up** with attendees after the event to keep the connection alive.

Real-Life Example:

A pet supply company sent their **staff** to a local adoption event, engaging with pet owners directly. The personal connection resulted in **50 new sign-ups** for their loyalty program, generating an additional **$1,000** in sales.

TIP 9: TRAIN STAFF TO SUBTLY INCORPORATE YOUR BUSINESS PITCH IN CONVERSATIONS

Well-trained staff can subtly promote your business during everyday conversations at events, making it feel natural rather than forced.

Why It Works:

- Staff can **build rapport** while naturally working your pitch into the conversation.
- Personal recommendations are often more effective than direct advertising.

How to Do It:

1. Train staff to look for **natural opportunities** to mention your business.
2. Teach them how to **build rapport** before introducing your product or service.
3. Keep the pitch **short and clear**, focusing on how your business can help the customer.

Real-Life Example:

A local bakery trained their staff to mention special deals during customer interactions at farmer's markets. This approach resulted in a **15%** increase in sales during market weekends.

TIP 10: PARTNER WITH LOCAL BUSINESSES TO SHARE BOOTH COSTS

Co-sharing booth space with a complementary local business can save both parties money while attracting new customers.

Why It Works:

- By sharing the costs of the booth, both businesses get exposure without doubling the expense.
- **Collaborative efforts** can attract more foot traffic, as customers may be drawn in by both brands.

How to Do It:

1. Reach out to complementary businesses (e.g., a coffee shop teaming up with a bookstore).
2. Split the cost of the booth, signage, and promotional materials.
3. Create joint offers to entice customers to visit both businesses.

Real-Life Example:

A small brewery teamed up with a local food truck to share booth space at a beer festival, cutting their booth fees in half. The partnership led to a **30%** increase in sales for both businesses.

5.
ADVERTISING ON APPAREL HACKS

TIP 1: UNIQUE, ATTENTION-GRABBING APPAREL WITH AI

Leverage AI tools to create custom designs that stand out on your apparel. These designs can be more creative and unique, giving your brand a fresh and innovative look.

Why It Works:

- **AI-generated designs** can produce one-of-a-kind graphics that attract attention and make your apparel more memorable.
- Tools like **Looka** or **Designify** can help generate logos, slogans, and graphic elements, saving time and money on hiring designers.

How to Do It:

1. Use AI design tools to create a few different designs based on your brand values.
2. Choose one design that will look great on your apparel, ensuring it's bold and eye-catching.
3. Print the design on various apparel items like t-shirts, hats, or tote bags.

Real-Life Example:

A startup clothing line used **AI-powered design tools** to create a custom logo for their apparel, which cost them **$50** for design and printing. The eye-catching design led to **200+ new orders**, totaling **$3,000 in revenue** during their first month.

TIP 2: PRINT IN BULK OR USE DIRECT-TO-GARMENT PRINTING FOR SMALL RUNS

Printing apparel in bulk or using **direct-to-garment** (DTG) printing is a cost-effective way to produce high-quality branded clothing.

Why It Works:

- **Bulk printing** reduces the per-unit cost, helping you save on every piece of apparel.
- **DTG printing** is ideal for small runs, allowing you to print designs without needing large inventory.

How to Do It:

1. Work with a local or online **bulk printer** to reduce printing costs.
2. For small runs, choose **DTG printing** to avoid setup fees and excess inventory.
3. Order in larger quantities to secure better pricing for future projects.

Real-Life Example:

A small boutique printed 500 t-shirts in bulk for an event, reducing the per-unit cost to **$5 per shirt**. After selling the shirts for **$20 each**, they generated **$7,500 in sales**, a significant return on their initial investment.

TIP 3: CREATE DUAL-PURPOSE DESIGNS (E.G., TOTE BAGS THAT ARE ALSO ADVERTISEMENTS)

Create designs for apparel that can serve a dual purpose, such as tote bags or hats that are not only functional but also advertise your brand.

Why It Works:

- **Dual-purpose items** are more likely to be used regularly, increasing your brand's exposure.
- People appreciate items that are both practical and branded, enhancing their perceived value.

How to Do It:

1. Create designs for **functional apparel** like hats, tote bags, or backpacks.
2. Make sure the design is **simple** but recognizable, acting as a walking advertisement.
3. Offer these items at affordable prices or as part of a giveaway to boost brand awareness.

Real-Life Example:

A local coffee shop designed branded tote bags and sold them for **$10 each**. The practical design led to **150 units** sold, increasing foot traffic and creating new regular customers who saw the bags used around town.

TIP 4: PARTNER WITH LOCAL INFLUENCERS TO WEAR AND PROMOTE YOUR BRANDED APPAREL

Leverage local influencers by providing them with branded apparel they can wear and promote on their social media channels.

Why It Works:

- **Influencers** can showcase your apparel to a targeted audience, driving interest and sales.
- Local influencers tend to have higher engagement rates with their community, which can lead to more genuine brand connections.

How to Do It:

1. Identify local influencers who align with your brand values.
2. Offer to provide them with **free apparel** in exchange for social media promotion.
3. Track the results through promo codes or affiliate links.

Real-Life Example:

A clothing brand partnered with a local **fashion influencer** who posted about their apparel on Instagram. The influencer's followers used a **custom promo code**, leading to **50 new orders** in just a week, increasing the brand's sales by **$1,000**.

TIP 5: FOCUS ON FUNCTIONAL ITEMS LIKE HATS OR HOODIES

Instead of investing in trendy, one-time-use items, focus on functional apparel that people will wear regularly, like hats, hoodies, and jackets.

Why It Works:

- **Functional items** have a longer lifespan and higher likelihood of being worn frequently, ensuring your brand is seen more often.
- These types of items are generally more popular and are perceived as higher value.

How to Do It:

1. Start by printing **branded hats** or **hoodies**, which are likely to be worn in various settings.
2. Choose colors and styles that appeal to your target demographic.
3. Ensure the design is subtle yet recognizable to build brand loyalty.

Real-Life Example:

A tech startup created **hoodies** with their logo, which became a hit among employees and their customers. The company distributed 100 hoodies at an event, and as a result, saw an **increase of 25% in brand recognition**.

TIP 6: OFFER APPAREL AS CONTEST PRIZES TO INCREASE VISIBILITY

Use your branded apparel as contest prizes to increase visibility and engagement with your audience.

Why It Works:

- Contests encourage people to engage with your brand and can generate organic **social media buzz**.
- Offering branded apparel as a prize is a **cost-effective** way to market your business.

How to Do It:

1. Run a **social media contest** where participants must follow your account, tag friends, or share your post.
2. Offer branded apparel as the prize to incentivize participation.
3. Use **hashtags** or **mentions** to encourage user-generated content and increase reach.

Real-Life Example:

A fitness studio ran a **Facebook contest** where participants could win a branded gym shirt by sharing their workout routines. The contest led to **200+ new followers** and a **10% boost** in sign-ups for their classes.

TIP 7: USE ONLINE PLATFORMS LIKE PRINTFUL FOR DROPSHIPPING APPAREL

If you don't want to hold inventory, use dropshipping platforms like **Printful** to print and ship apparel on-demand.

Why It Works:

- **Printful** and similar services handle the printing, packaging, and shipping, which saves you time and reduces overhead costs.
- This model allows you to **test new designs** without the risk of holding stock.

How to Do It:

1. Set up an **online store** with Printful or a similar platform.
2. Upload your designs and select which apparel items you want to offer.
3. When a customer places an order, the platform will handle everything, and you get a **percentage** of the sale.

Real-Life Example:

A lifestyle brand used **Printful** to dropship branded shirts and hats. They didn't have to invest in inventory, and their designs earned them **$2,000** in profits during their first month with no upfront costs.

TIP 8: START WITH COST-EFFECTIVE T-SHIRTS BEFORE EXPANDING TO OTHER ITEMS

T-shirts are inexpensive and versatile, making them a great starting point for your apparel marketing efforts.

Why It Works:

- **T-shirts** are cost-effective and can be sold or given away at events for maximum exposure.
- They're also **universally popular** and can easily fit any brand style.

How to Do It:

1. Start by printing **branded t-shirts** with your logo and a simple, eye-catching design.
2. Test the market to see what resonates with your audience.
3. Once you've found a successful design, expand to other items like hoodies or hats.

Real-Life Example:

A local brewery started by selling **branded t-shirts** for **$12** each. The shirts were a hit, and after selling **500 units**, they expanded their product line to include **$25 hoodies**, earning another **$3,000**.

TIP 9: CHOOSE COLORS AND DESIGNS THAT APPEAL TO YOUR TARGET DEMOGRAPHIC

Your apparel design and colors should appeal to your audience's tastes and preferences to maximize engagement.

Why It Works:

- Choosing the right **colors** and **designs** helps ensure that your apparel is appealing and wearable, increasing the chances it will be seen in public.
- Consider the psychology of color when designing to attract your ideal customers.

How to Do It:

1. Research your target demographic to understand which colors, styles, and designs appeal to them.
2. Choose **bold colors** for impact or **neutral tones** for versatility.
3. Tailor your designs to reflect your audience's interests, values, and aesthetics.

Real-Life Example:

A local yoga studio created **simple yet elegant t-shirts** in muted pastel colors. The shirts sold out quickly, generating over **$1,500** in sales in just one month, and they gained a loyal following.

TIP 10: ORGANIZE A BRANDED APPAREL GIVEAWAY AT LOCAL EVENTS

Give away your branded apparel at local events to increase exposure and build a community around your brand.

Why It Works:

- **Free giveaways** at events increase brand recognition and create goodwill among potential customers.
- Attendees who receive free apparel are more likely to **wear it** and **advertise** your brand.

How to Do It:

1. Attend local events or set up a booth at a popular festival or market.
2. Offer free apparel to event-goers in exchange for following your brand on social media or sharing your post.
3. Track the impact by asking people to tag your business when they wear your apparel.

Real-Life Example:

A local restaurant hosted a **giveaway event** at a food festival, where they gave away 100 branded t-shirts. The giveaway led to an increase of **200 new social media followers** and a **15% increase** in foot traffic during the following month.

6.
VEHICLE AND HIGH-TRAFFIC AREA ADVERTISING HACKS

TIP 1: TRANSFORM YOUR VEHICLE INTO A MOBILE BILLBOARD

Your vehicle is the ultimate **mobile advertisement** that can go anywhere. Wrapping your car, truck, or trailer with bold, eye-catching graphics allows you to take your brand wherever you drive, maximizing your exposure without any extra effort.

Why It Works:

- Constant visibility, especially in **high-traffic areas**.
- **Non-intrusive**—people see your ad while they go about their day.
- A **long-term investment** that continues to work for you.

How to Do It:

- Wrap your vehicle with a **vibrant design** featuring your business name, contact details, and a call to action.
- Use **partial wraps** to cut costs but still maximize the visibility of key information.
- If a full wrap is not feasible, **vinyl decals** or **magnets** are great cost-effective alternatives.

Real-Life Example:

A **local cleaning service** turned their van into a **mobile billboard** by wrapping it with vibrant, eye-catching graphics that showcased their services and contact info. The van was regularly parked in busy areas like shopping malls and business districts. As a result, they saw a **25% increase in calls** and **a noticeable boost in online inquiries** from local customers who had seen the van driving around or parked in high-traffic areas.

TIP 2: UTILIZE DIGITAL BILLBOARDS NEAR BUSY INTERSECTIONS

If you're looking for a modern take on traditional billboard advertising, consider **digital billboards** along high-traffic roads or intersections. These billboards can display dynamic content that grabs attention as drivers pass by.

Why It Works:

- Digital billboards can **rotate ads** frequently, giving you the chance to update your message or run time-sensitive promotions.
- **Targeted reach** in high-traffic areas where people can see your ad repeatedly.
- **Cost-effective** compared to traditional static billboards with the ability to reach more people in shorter intervals.

How to Do It:

- Find digital billboards in **busy traffic areas** or highways.
- Create a **bold, easy-to-read design** with a strong call to action.
- **Test different messages** over time to see which resonates best with the audience.

Real-Life Example:

A fitness center used digital billboards to advertise limited-time offers and membership discounts. They targeted busy streets near gyms, and within a few weeks, they saw **20% more new memberships**.

TIP 3: CO-ADVERTISE ON PARKING LOT ADS

Leverage the space in busy **parking lots** by partnering with local businesses to share parking lot ads. These ads could include posters or large banners that sit near the entrance or along high-traffic areas where cars park.

Why It Works:

- A **low-cost solution** that still gets good visibility.
- Directly targets customers **arriving or leaving** high-traffic retail locations, especially those with a long dwell time.
- **Shared costs** with another business make it affordable.

How to Do It:

- Identify parking lots near your business or complementary businesses that attract your target market.
- Work with local property managers to install large **banners or posters** at high-visibility points.
- Consider partnering with nearby businesses to split costs for a larger, more impactful ad.

Real-Life Example:

A local restaurant partnered with a nearby clothing store to place banners at the entrance of their parking lot. The shared cost was **$300** for a month, resulting in a **15% increase in foot traffic** for both businesses.

TIP 4: USE TRAILER ADS IN BUSY AREAS WITH HEAVY VEHICLE TRAFFIC

If you have access to a **trailer**, park it strategically in areas with heavy vehicle traffic, such as near busy intersections or local events. Trailer advertising provides a large, visible surface for your brand message.

Why It Works:

- **Large surface area** gives you plenty of room for your brand message and imagery.
- **Stationary advertising** in a high-traffic area means people will see your ad repeatedly.
- You can use your trailer for **multiple types of promotions** by swapping out signage.

How to Do It:

- Wrap your trailer with a **bold design** that showcases your business name, logo, and contact info.
- Park in **high-traffic zones** like construction sites, shopping centers, or event venues where there's continuous vehicle movement.
- Rotate the trailer to different locations to maximize visibility.

Real-Life Example:

A landscaping company parked their branded trailer at a popular shopping center during the weekends. The large, easily visible wrap resulted in a **25% increase in local inquiries**.

TIP 5: USE CAR MAGNET ADVERTISING AT BUSY EVENTS

If you don't want a full vehicle wrap, **magnetic signs** are a great solution. You can place these on the sides of your car or truck and take them off when not in use. This is especially effective at **local events**, street fairs, or markets where there's a high concentration of vehicles.

Why It Works:

- **Cost-effective** compared to full wraps.
- **Flexibility** to remove and move the ad to various locations.
- **High exposure** in busy areas where large crowds gather.

How to Do It:

- Create large, **bold magnetic signs** with your branding and a short call to action.
- Display them during **local events** or in parking lots with high foot traffic.
- Move the car or truck between busy locations like markets, festivals, or sports events.

Real-Life Example:

A local ice cream truck used magnetic signs with their logo and a special discount offer for a weekend festival. The magnetic sign cost them **$50**, but they saw a **40% increase in sales** during the event.

TIP 6: TEMPORARY STREET SIGNAGE FOR STREET CORNERS

If you can't park your vehicle in one place for long periods, consider placing **temporary street signs** on corners or sidewalks near major intersections or busy roads. These signs can direct passing traffic to your location or offer limited-time promotions.

Why It Works:

- **Highly visible**—drivers, pedestrians, and cyclists will see the sign from afar.
- **Affordable** compared to billboards or digital ads.
- Effective in directing customers who are already in the area to your business.

How to Do It:

- Design a **clear, eye-catching sign** that includes your business name, location, and a strong call to action.
- Make sure the sign is **durable** enough to withstand weather if it's outdoors for extended periods.
- Place the signs in **strategic spots** near high-traffic areas, such as intersections, bus stops, or near popular retail stores.

Real-Life Example:

A local coffee shop used bright street signs directing people from a busy intersection to their shop a few blocks away. The **$100** they spent on signage resulted in a **10% increase in foot traffic** that week.

TIP 7: USE CAR WRAPS IN PARKING GARAGES

Parking garages in **busy city centers** and shopping malls provide a unique opportunity for advertising. Vehicles in these spaces, especially in high-traffic areas of the garage, can be used to display large, attention-grabbing wraps.

Why It Works:

- **Consistent visibility** as cars are parked in high-traffic areas of the garage.
- **Affordable parking rates** make it cost-effective for advertisers.
- **Close proximity** to shopping centers or office buildings means people are already in the area and more likely to act on the ad.

How to Do It:

- Partner with **parking garages** to allow your vehicle to be parked in high-traffic sections.
- Apply a **full vehicle wrap** with vibrant, easy-to-read information.
- Make sure your ad stands out by using **bold graphics** or adding a **QR code** for easy access to your website.

Real-Life Example:

A tech company used a **bright blue car wrap** in a parking garage near an office district. The exposure led to **15% more website visits** from people who noticed the wrap while walking by.

TIP 8: ADVERTISE ON GAS STATION PUMPS

Gas stations are prime real estate for reaching drivers, especially those who frequent the same locations. Advertising on **gas pump screens** or having **ads on the gas pump itself** allows you to target drivers when they're filling up, a captive audience with time to read your message.

Why It Works:

- **High dwell time**—drivers often spend 3-5 minutes at the pump.
- **Localized targeting**—ads can be shown at specific stations where your target audience frequents.
- **Affordable**—costs are typically lower than other forms of outdoor advertising, like billboards.

How to Do It:

- Partner with local gas stations to place **ads on digital screens** or even print ads on the pump itself.
- Create an **eye-catching design** with a clear call to action.
- Consider adding a **discount code** or special offer for drivers to redeem at your business.

Real-Life Example:

A local **pizza chain** used ads on gas pump screens near office parks to promote their **delivery service** with a discount. The result: a **20% increase in online orders** within a month.

TIP 9: FLASHING LED SIGNS IN TRAFFIC CONGESTION ZONES

During rush hour or traffic congestion, **flashing LED signs** that display rotating ads can capture the attention of drivers. These signs can be strategically placed in areas where traffic tends to slow down or stop, such as near traffic lights, tollbooths, or accident-prone spots.

Why It Works:

- **Captive audience**—drivers are forced to stop or slow down, giving them time to read your ad.
- **High visibility**—LED lights ensure your ad stands out even in low-light conditions.
- **Attention-grabbing**—flashing lights and movement make it harder for drivers to ignore.

How to Do It:

- Work with local traffic authorities or private businesses to place flashing LED signs at key intersections or areas with frequent congestion.
- Create a **simple and direct message** with a call to action that can be read quickly.
- Consider **rotating ads** or using humor to capture attention.

Real-Life Example:

A **car dealership** placed flashing LED signs at a busy intersection to advertise their **sale**. The outcome: a **15% increase in showroom visits** over the following month.

TIP 10: CAR WINDOW STICKERS FOR HIGH-VALUE AREAS

A fun little sticker can go a long way. This method works well in areas with heavy pedestrian traffic, as people walking by can easily spot the ads on vehicles parked in these areas.

Why It Works:

- **Highly visible**—easily seen by pedestrians and other drivers.
- **Cost-effective**—cheap to produce, especially when ordered in bulk.
- **Customizable**—you can use creative designs, catchy slogans, or QR codes to engage viewers.

How to Do It:

- Design small, colorful stickers with your **brand name**, **contact info**, or a **promo offer**.
- Place them on cars in high-traffic parking lots, preferably near **targeted locations** like shopping malls, office complexes, or event centers.
- Offer drivers an **incentive** for displaying the sticker, like discounts or a prize, to increase participation.

Real-Life Example:

A **fitness center** distributed branded window decals to members, offering discounts for displaying them on cars. This led to a **30% increase in membership sign-ups**.

7.
BUSINESS CARDS AND POSTCARDS HACKS

TIP 1: KEEP BUSINESS CARD DESIGNS SIMPLE TO REDUCE PRINTING COSTS

By keeping your business card designs clean and minimal, you can save on **printing costs**. Avoid intricate designs and overly complex elements that might require special inks or finishes.

Why It Works:

- **Lower production cost** due to simple designs.
- **Faster printing turnaround** because of reduced complexity.

How to Do It:

- Use basic fonts and colors to avoid additional charges for special designs.
- Limit the amount of information—just your essentials (name, job title, contact details).
- Opt for standard card sizes (3.5" x 2") to avoid custom cutting costs.

Real-Life Example:

A **local consultant** streamlined their business card design by using a simple logo and basic contact info, cutting their printing costs by **30%** while still making a professional impact.

TIP 2: USE DOUBLE-SIDED CARDS TO PACK MORE INFO WITHOUT NEEDING ADDITIONAL MATERIALS

A **double-sided business card** allows you to include more details without increasing the overall cost or requiring additional pieces. Use the back for extra info like services or social media handles.

Why It Works:

- **Maximizes space** without increasing cost.
- **Efficient**—you don't need separate materials for additional info.

How to Do It:

- Use the back for additional details that don't need to be on the front, like services, promotions, or QR codes.
- Avoid cluttering the front with too much information— keep it clean and professional.

Real-Life Example:

A **freelance web designer** used double-sided cards to list services on the back, leading to an **increase in client inquiries** because prospects could easily see what they offer.

TIP 3: CREATE INTERACTIVE POSTCARDS WITH PERFORATED COUPONS OR DISCOUNTS

Including **perforated coupons** or discounts on postcards makes them more valuable and interactive. This encourages recipients to keep the postcard and take action.

Why It Works:

- **Higher engagement**—people love to use discounts.
- **Cost-effective**—adds value without significant added expense.

How to Do It:

- Offer a **discount coupon** or **freebie** on a perforated section of the postcard.
- Make sure the offer is time-sensitive to encourage quick action.
- Ensure the coupon has a **clear call-to-action** (e.g., "Present this card for 10% off!").

Real-Life Example:

A **local restaurant** used postcards with a perforated coupon offering a free appetizer, resulting in **50% more foot traffic** during the campaign period.

TIP 4: USE AI TO REFINE BUSINESS CARD LAYOUTS FOR MAXIMUM CLARITY

AI tools like **Canva** or **Looka** can help you design business cards with a clean, professional layout, ensuring your contact info is clear and easily readable.

Why It Works:

- **Quick and easy**—AI tools automate the design process.
- **Improved clarity**—ensures the design looks professional without clutter.

How to Do It:

- Use an **AI design tool** like Canva or Looka to generate business card layouts.
- Select templates that highlight essential information and leave space for key elements.
- Ensure your **contact info** is easily readable and not overcrowded.

Real-Life Example:

An **entrepreneur** used an AI tool to create a sleek business card with an optimized layout, leading to **positive feedback** from clients impressed by the professional design.

TIP 5: TRY NONTRADITIONAL CARD SHAPES TO STAND OUT (E.G., ROUNDED EDGES)

Opt for **rounded edge cards** or other unique shapes that help your business card stand out. A unique card design can make a lasting impression.

Why It Works:

- **Memorable**—stands out from typical rectangular cards.
- **Increases brand recall** because of the unique shape.

How to Do It:

- Choose a **unique shape** like rounded edges, square cards, or custom cuts to create a standout look.
- Use the unique shape as part of your branding, aligning it with your business identity.
- Be sure that your design still allows for readability and functionality despite the nontraditional shape.

Real-Life Example:

A **boutique marketing agency** used rounded business cards that matched their branding, leading to **more referrals** from clients who found the cards unique and memorable.

TIP 6: PRINT ON RECYCLED MATERIALS FOR COST-EFFECTIVENESS AND SUSTAINABILITY

Printing on **recycled materials** is often cheaper and more sustainable than traditional materials. It also communicates your commitment to sustainability, which can be appealing to customers.

Why It Works:

- **Lower cost**—recycled materials are often less expensive.
- **Eco-friendly**—appeals to environmentally conscious clients.

How to Do It:

- Check with your **printer** about recycled options like post-consumer paper or eco-friendly inks.
- Use these materials for both business cards and postcards to maintain consistency in your sustainability efforts.

Real-Life Example:

A **local eco-friendly cleaning business** printed their business cards on recycled paper, reducing costs by **20%** while aligning with their green brand values.

TIP 7: USE AUGMENTED REALITY (AR) CODES TO MAKE YOUR CARDS INTERACTIVE

Integrate **AR codes** on your business cards that lead to an interactive experience, such as a video introduction or a link to your portfolio.

Why It Works:

- **High-tech appeal**—AR adds a futuristic touch.
- **Engaging**—creates a memorable experience for potential clients.

How to Do It:

- Include an **AR code** on your business card that links to a specific digital experience (like a portfolio, product demo, or welcome message).
- Use tools like **Zappar** or **Layar** to create AR codes.
- Ensure that the **link or experience** is mobile-friendly and accessible.

Real-Life Example:

A **tech startup** included an AR code on their business cards that led to a product demo video, increasing the **number of product trials** by 40%.

TIP 8: DESIGN REUSABLE PROMOTIONAL POSTCARDS FOR MULTIPLE CAMPAIGNS

Create postcards that can be used for different campaigns by keeping the design generic but with space for **customizable details** like dates, offers, or events.

Why It Works:

- **Cost-effective**—print once, reuse for future promotions.
- **Flexible**—easy to modify for different campaigns.

How to Do It:

- Use a **clean, general design** for the front (e.g., logo, brand colors, and slogan) and leave space for hand-written details or printed info.
- Ensure that the details like dates, offers, or event locations can easily be added or updated.

Real-Life Example:

A **real estate agent** printed reusable postcards with space for handwritten details like property information, allowing them to use the same postcards for multiple listings, saving on printing costs.

TIP 9: LIMIT THE NUMBER OF COLORS TO REDUCE PRINTING EXPENSES

Using fewer colors in your business card and postcard design can drastically reduce printing costs. Stick to **two or three colors** for a clean and affordable design.

Why It Works:

- **Reduces printing costs**—fewer colors mean less expensive ink and material usage.
- **Simplicity**—a limited color palette can look professional and elegant.

How to Do It:

- Limit your color scheme to **two or three** shades that represent your brand.
- Opt for **black and white** designs with one accent color to keep the look sleek but affordable.

Real-Life Example:

A **local law firm** used a simple **black-and-white design** for their business cards, cutting their printing costs by **15%** while maintaining a sleek, professional image.

TIP 10: USE YOUR CARDS AS MINI PORTFOLIOS BY INCLUDING A SMALL DESIGN SAMPLE OR QR CODE

Turn your business cards into **mini portfolios** by adding a small sample of your work or a QR code linking to your website, portfolio, or social media.

Why It Works:

- **Showcases your work** — gives clients a direct way to view what you do.
- **Convenient** — QR codes make it easy to access your digital portfolio.

How to Do It:

- Include a **small portfolio piece** (e.g., a design snippet, a photo of your work) on the back or front of the card.
- Add a **QR code** linking to your portfolio, social media, or website.

Real-Life Example:

A **graphic designer** added a QR code to their business cards that led to their online portfolio, which led to **more client inquiries** and a higher conversion rate.

8.
THE ROAD AHEAD

FINAL THOUGHTS

As we've explored throughout this book, small savings can quickly add up to significant results for your business. Whether it's cutting costs on design, leveraging free tools, or finding creative ways to reach your audience, every little change can make a big impact. By applying the strategies shared here, you can reduce unnecessary expenses while still delivering effective marketing and design that drives results.

The key to success in marketing is staying creative and flexible. The business landscape is always evolving, and the most successful entrepreneurs are those who remain adaptable and open to exploring new methods. Don't hesitate to think outside the box and experiment with innovative, cost-effective tools—many of which are free or low-cost. This approach allows you to grow your business without compromising on quality.

As your business evolves, so will your marketing needs. Revisit these tips as you continue to expand and refine your strategies. The most successful businesses thrive by continuously learning and applying new ideas to their existing plans. By staying informed and innovative, you'll be equipped to save money while achieving your business goals.

At PoweredUpWeb.com, we're always here to support busy business owners who need guidance. If you're feeling overwhelmed or need advice, don't hesitate to reach out. We're happy to offer free advice and help you make the most of the tools and strategies available. Thank you for taking this journey with me. I hope these tips empower you to save money, streamline your marketing efforts, and achieve your goals.

FEATURED RESOURCES

This book mentions several tools, websites, and platforms designed to help you save time and money in your marketing and design efforts. Below is a complete list, along with some additional recommendations to explore.

Digital Marketing
- **Google Keyword Planner**: Find the best keywords to target for your campaigns. https://ads.google.com
- **ChatGPT**: Generate ad copy, blog posts, and more with AI assistance. https://openai.com
- **Buffer**: Schedule and manage social media posts effortlessly. https://buffer.com
- **Carrd**: Create free, simple landing pages. https://carrd.co
- **Mailchimp**: Manage email campaigns with easy-to-use tools. https://mailchimp.com
-

Digital Design
- **Canva**: Design professional graphics without any prior experience. https://www.canva.com
- **Looka**: AI-powered logo and branding creation. https://looka.com
- **Unsplash**: Access free, high-quality stock photos. https://unsplash.com
- **Designify**: Enhance your images and designs quickly. https://designify.com

Print Marketing
- **Vistaprint**: Affordable printing for business cards, postcards, and more. https://vistaprint.com

- **GotPrint**: Another budget-friendly option for printing business materials. https://gotprint.com

Vehicle Advertising
- **Local Vinyl Wrap Shops**: Search for certified installers in your area for custom vehicle wraps.
- **Affordable Car Magnets and Vinyl**: Affordable magnetic and vinyl prints for vehicles. https://signs.com

Additional Recommendations
- **AppSumo**: Get lifetime deals on marketing and design software. https://appsumo.com
- **SendFox**: If Mailchimp is not your thing, go with SendFox and only pay once. https://sendfox.com/
- **Zapier**: Automate workflows and lead generation. https://zapier.com
- **Fiverr**: Affordable freelancing for design, copywriting, and more. https://fiverr.com
- **Printful**: Print and dropship custom apparel and merchandise. https://printful.com

These resources have been tested by countless businesses, including myself and clients of Powered Up Web. Explore them to find the best fit for your unique needs!

ABOUT THE AUTHOR

Hi there! I'm Hajrudin Spiodic, the proud owner of Powered Up Web. My mission is simple: to help small businesses and startups grow through affordable, high-quality marketing and design services. Over the years, PoweredUpWeb.com has supported countless clients with web development, social media management, design, and business advising, always with a focus on results and cost-effectiveness.

But let me tell you, my journey here wasn't all smooth sailing. I've started and failed more times than I can count. Those experiences taught me what works, what doesn't, and how to stretch a budget without cutting corners. I've used just about every advertising platform you can imagine, so when I share advice, it comes from years of trial, error, and success.

When I'm not helping businesses thrive, I love spending time with my family or making music just for fun. Life's about balance, and I'm lucky to have found mine. I hope this book inspires you to grow your business without breaking the bank—and remember, Powered Up Web is always here to help!